MW01290159

HEALTHY RECIPE FOR
MARRIAGE
UNITY

HEALTHY RECIPE FOR

MARRIAGE
UNITY

*GOD'S WORD PREPARES MARRIAGE Then the
Lord God said, "It is not good that the man should be
alone. I will make him a helper fit for him."*
Genesis 2:18

MS. MARION OATES

XULON PRESS

Xulon Press
2301 Lucien Way #415
Maitland, FL 32751
407.339.4217
www.xulonpress.com

© 2020 by Ms. Marion Oates

All rights reserved solely by the author. The author guarantees all contents are original and do not infringe upon the legal rights of any other person or work. No part of this book may be reproduced in any form without the permission of the author. The views expressed in this book are not necessarily those of the publisher.

Unless otherwise indicated, Scripture quotations taken from the King James Version (KJV) – *public domain.*

Paperback ISBN-13: 978-1-6628-0261-4
Ebook ISBN-13: 978-1-6628-0262-1

Table of Contents

Chapter Ten

Author's Preface

This book is written to educate and ensure that pre-marital and married couples understand the significance of accepting God as a part of their everyday lives. When God is absent from your life, especially in marriage, you are fighting your own battles. You may think you are doing well on your own, but only God can dictate that. He is your rock in times of need.

The Holy Spirit, who guides with wisdom and understanding, led me to write this book for couples who are pursuing marriage, to share how important it is to keep God in their lives. I am hopeful that my experiences will help to guide you in the right direction so your marriage will be long-lasting. Later in the book, I will share some of my experiences. Marriage will not always be perfect; however, with God's help, it can be a blessing. God is merciful, kind, and just, and He will not give up on you.

During the COVID-19 pandemic, I was secluded within the privacy of my quiet home, away from the outside world, and I started writing. I had more time to study the Bible while attending church on Zoom.

Besides writing, I spent time watching Christian movies for relaxation and to grow in humbleness. Despite what has been happening in the outside world, God has kept me at peace. Writing a book on relationships was extremely exciting to me. This was an interesting subject for me because I longed to think of ways to educate couples with the hope of securing both married and premarital couples to work on developing lasting relationships. My intention is to inspire couples with ways to unite with God, making Him the Lord of their lives. When I was husband hunting on my own, unity with God was the missing link in my life, and I ended up marrying and divorcing three times. God is not fond of divorce. During that time, I was leaning to my own understanding. Proverbs 3:5 says, "Trust in the Lord with all your heart, and lean not to your own understanding."

I was passionate about writing this book because I wanted to share my experiences. Someone asked me, "Do you really want to talk about your past?" I responded, "Why not?" I must be transparent with my readers and share that I am not perfect. They will see that I have a story to tell. Many times, people marry for the wrong reasons or marry the wrong person, which usually happens when they are not allowing God to lead them. God wants you to allow Him to help you with decisions so your marriage can be successful and long-lasting.

As I stated previously, after I had observed many separated and divorced couples, the Holy Spirit led me to inform couples of the missing link in their lives. Most times, couples divorce because of lack of commitment, constant arguing, infidelity, marrying too young or too soon, unrealistic expectations, abuse, and so on... When your marriage is in chaos, God is not pleased because He does not like confusion. Marriage cannot survive on cruelty, disrespect, inconsiderateness, or abusive behavior to each other. While marriage will never be perfect, however, if it is handled a way that is pleasing to God, it can be exceptional. Prayer is necessity in keep couples together. Simply depend on your Lord and Savior to help you, and your marriage will work out. Just as a plant needs watering, your marriage needs this as well, or it will die.

What does the Bible say about marriage? The Bible states that God instituted marriage in the Garden of Eden at the time of man's creation, as a union between man and woman. Marriage is a basic social institution that has been around for as far back as we have historical records—in both secular sources and the Bible—although it has taken different forms at different times and in different cultures. When God created marriage, He meant for two to become one flesh. "Therefore, a man shall leave his father and mother and be joined to his wife, and they shall become one flesh" (Gen. 2:22-24).

Introduction

My Story: Nineteen and Pregnant

Hello, readers. I would like to begin my story. I will be transparent in giving you highlights of my previous marriages. During this time in my life, I was not leaning on God. If I had desired God in my life, He would have guided me away from getting involved with the wrong person.

This is the first time I have shared my story with anyone. However, I feel a need to share it with my readers so you can understand what I have been through. My intentions are to keep anyone else from going through what I went through. I am not perfect, and neither are you. Romans 3:23 says, "For all have sinned and fall short of the glory of God."

I have been married and divorced three times. I am not proud of being divorced that many times. If I could start over again and include God in my life, I believe that I would have been in a better place in my journey. God is now the head of my life and He has sent me a godly husband.. My story is forthcoming.

Highlights on first marriage

I was nineteen and pregnant when I first got married to a man who was six years older than me. When I married at such a young age, I did not know anything about love at that age. Even though I remained married for a long time, I had never fallen in love with my husband. There were several reasons why I could not fall in love with him; first, I got married too soon and for the wrong reason. I wanted to be on my own, so when he asked me to marry him, I decided to. Little did I know, I was making a mistake. Nevertheless, I bore four children during this marriage. He was a good father to our children, but he was very domineering, jealous, and abusive to me.

We got married and had a big wedding. Before the wedding, I did not have a chance to get to know him because I married too fast. He was not the best at communicating. This was a big flaw for me because communication is the key for me. We were not evenly yoked, which is a must in order to have a good marriage. God was not in the midst. Also, I did not know my husband was a big drinker. I eventually found out he was very jealous as well as abusive, and besides that, he was very sexually active outside the home, having many children other than the four we had together.

Finally, after nineteen years, I decided to divorce him. Check this out: I got married at nineteen and divorced nineteen years later. I said, "how ironic?" So, I decided to take my four children and get away from all the drama. I was afraid of him because he was abusive, so our marriage came down to a divorce, which I never wanted to have because I knew God frowned on divorce. After my divorce, I stayed unmarried for more than ten years.

Highlights on second marriage

Following those years, I decided to marry again. I did not seek God in this second marriage either. This time, I met this gentleman at the bowling alley actually I was introduced by a relative of his. We both were avid bowlers. I was introduced and we started dating. After dating for months, he asked me if I would let him move in with me, saying he could help me around the house and he was a great handyman. I told him that he could help me with my house, but I would not live with him unless we were married. Well, his response was, "That can be arranged." I said, "Wow!" I knew he was not in love with me, so we just dated a while longer. Finally, I conceded and agreed to marry him.

Within five years of our marriage, he started seeing other women. We were married for a total of ten years. We stayed together for five years and then separated for the next five years. However, during those first five years of marriage, he broke our vows and defiled the marriage. He started doing things out of the ordinary. For example, he used to call me every day, two to three times a day, then he changed his routine and called only when he felt like it. He became more and more bold with his actions, and I found out he was cheating on me. I even suggested pastoral counseling and sector counseling. At the counseling session, when he was asked what he wanted to do to save his marriage and if he would be willing to leave any outside distraction to devote time for his marriage, he responded, "I don't know." Well, you know how that made me feel. The counselor told me that he would be glad to finish counseling me, but he could not help him. So, I made up my mind that I could not take it any longer, being married to a man who do not want to change to make the marriage better. So, unfortunately, another divorce ensued. Thank God we did not have any children in this marriage. After the demise of my marriage, I moved on.

Highlights on third marriage

I will now tell you about my third marriage, which also took place without God in it. This time, the dating game came into play on the Internet, where I met this gentleman. He told me he wanted to get married! Not long after we had started dating, he proposed to me on his knees. I thought that was so romantic. At this point in my life, I was looking for someone who liked to travel, not particularly love because up to this point love was not working. He said he liked to travel, but his idea of travel was going fishing on his bass boat, which he took *very seriously. As far as he was concerned, if I wanted to go with him, fine, but if I did not, that was fine also. It turned out that he was claiming to be a "professional fisherman." He was so involved in his fishing that he really did not have time for me. I could walk past him in the nude, and he would not even notice. My thought was that he only wanted companionship, not a wife.*

So, I started feeling way unloved, lonely, and craving attention. Therefore, I decided to give the marriage a year, then ask for a divorce. We were married for one year, and that is when our marriage ended. I told my husband I did not get married to stay single.

Of course, I can blame myself. Everything I am sharing with you is what I should have been mature enough to know and understand and less naïve and gullible and that is why I needed God in my life and so do you. You should never get married unless you are in love. Through all my marriages, I learned the hard way while it just does not pay to get married unless it is for love—and unconditional love at that! Three failed marriages, and God was not pleased.

I have repented for my failed marriages. God intended for marriage to be until death do us part. After those three marriages, I realized it was time to seek God in everything. Had I done that before my first marriage, there would not have been three. I suffered needlessly in my previous marriages because I was young, immature, naïve, and I married for all the wrong reasons. I had always wanted to be married; I did not give God a second thought. Because of this, my marriages dissolved in mental distress, heartache, and pain, which could have been avoided. I tolerated a lot in my three marriages because, unknowingly, I stepped out of the path God had planned for me. Lessons learned!

I prayed for God to send me a godly, spiritual man to be my husband. I asked Him for a good man who loved Him and knew how to treat a wife, someone who would love me unconditionally. So, I just waited on God until He moved. While being patient God sent me that special someone, just what I asked for! Philippians 4:13 says, "I can do all things through Jesus Christ who strengthens me."

As you can see from my stories, God is the perfect recipe for me. Marriage is a covenant with God and a contract between three people: God, a husband, and a wife. What a great recipe in a marriage covenant! Couples, God is important to have in your life. Hence, you can begin a marriage with good intentions at its conception, but if you don't start out with God's help, there is no guarantee you will not run into problems later on that you can't fix on your own. Just as I did, many couples get married for the wrong reasons, and many ends up in divorce court. As you saw in my stories, I experienced divorce because I chose to follow my own intuition instead of allowing God to work in my life.

If you do your marriage right (and by right, I mean with God), divorce should not be an option.

In the Bible, marriage is the act of uniting a man and a woman for life; it is wedlock, or the legal union of a man and a woman for life. Marriage is a contract both civil and religious, by which two parties engage to live together in mutual affection and fidelity, until death shall separate them. God Himself instituted marriage for the purpose of preventing the promiscuous intercourse of the sexes, for promoting domestic felicity, and for securing the maintenance and education of children. He created the husband and the wife equally, and He ordained them to "become one," a biblical principle He first ordained in Genesis 2:24, which Jesus reaffirmed in Matthew 19:4-6 and Mark 10:6-8, and Apostle Paul reinforced in Ephesians 5:30-32. Mark 10:6-9 tells us, "But from the beginning of the creation, God made them male and female. For this cause, shall a man leave his father and mother, and cleave to his wife, and they twain shall be one flesh'; so, they are no more twain, but one flesh. What therefore, God has joined together, let not man put asunder." Hebrew 13:4 says, "Marriage is honorable in all and the bed undefiled."

Beware of false love. Infatuation can often feel like true love. In "The Real Difference Between

Infatuation and Love," [1]Amanda Chatel shares that there is a big difference between infatuation and love. Infatuation is when you first see someone you are attracted to and immediately feel there is a connection based on that, whereas love is knowing the good and bad of someone and still loving them all the same.

When you first meet someone and you are really smitten with them, it can be hard to tell if you are in love, falling in love, or merely experiencing infatuation. Love and infatuation feel remarkably similar. Infatuation is short in duration, while love weathers the storm and continues to grow. Love forgives and understands, but infatuation does not. For example, when you get married and start having troubles in your marriage, there is a tendency to separate or divorce because the love was not unconditional. That is when you know it was not true love. However, true or unconditional love, also known as Agape love, will last because couples are willing to work through their issues with prayer, discussion, and counseling to stay married. When you know the difference between love and infatuation, you will not likely make a mistake, and you will be able to discern the truth of the relationship. Here are some differences between infatuation and love: *infatuation* is immediate and steeped in fantasy, and *love* takes time and

---
[1] Chatel, Amanda, "The Real Differences between Infatuation and Love"

is grounded in reality; *infatuation* creates perfection, and *love* is about evolving together; *infatuation* is a sea of illusions, making us seek perfection in ourselves, and *love* makes us real.

Simply speaking, when you are deep in love, you will fight for your marriage. The way to become deep in love is through prayer and leaning on God for His help. I know this because I am a three-time divorcee, having made decisions without God and prayer during my life's endeavors.

Thanks to my Lord and Savior, my last and only marriage, which I am in right now, is wonderful. He answered my prayer and gave me this wonderful husband. Divorce is not an option anymore.

The following is Sister Muriel Bynum's testimony on marriage. She speaks about the question, "What does it take to make a successful marriage?"

My testimony is that there is no one sure, tried-and-true way to guarantee that a marriage will have perfection from start to finish. Our own human nature prevents that because we are not perfect beings. There are several generic sayings, such as "marriage is give and take," "marriage takes sacrifice," and "marriage is 50/50." All of these are true to some extent. After nearly thirty-five years of marriage, I have come to the following conclusions: marriage is give and take—more giving and less taking. The selfishness of the human spirit makes us automatically want more than we receive because we feel we are entitled for all our hard work. However, marriage takes sacrifice; it depends on who is doing all the sacrificing, which leads me to my last point.

"Marriage is 50/50" is hogwash, nonsense, foolishness. Marriage is a 100 percent effort from both sides. You cannot wait around for someone to fill the rest of the relationship, just because you think you have given your 50 percent. If both people are pushing at full throttle 100 percent and expecting nothing in return, can you imagine the power in the strength of the relationship?

What a wonderful and honest testimony from a Christian woman who has been married for thirty-five years. She elaborates on what it takes to have a good marriage with God in control. Aside from having God in your life, it is essential that you and your spouse do all you can to sustain your marriage. Of course, you cannot do anything without God; there is little we can do by ourselves. So, we must trust Him. As I previously shared, Proverbs 3:5-6 says, "Trust in the Lord with all thine heart; and lean not unto thine own understanding; In all your ways acknowledge Him, and He shall direct thy paths."

We must understand that marriage will have its ups and downs, but we must have faith in God, knowing He will help us to stay faithful and committed through those tough times, no matter what happens. Thank you, and I hope this book will be helpful to you!

Chapter One

God's Design for Marriage

What is the purpose of marriage? The Bible has a lot to say about this topic. According to "Biblical Perspective on Marriage"[2] from *Crosswalk.com*,[3] Christian marriages are to reflect God's image. Genesis 1:26-27 says, "Then God said, 'Let us make in our image, according to our likeness: let them have dominion over the fish of the sea, over the birds of the air, over the livestock, over all the earth, and over every creeping thing that creeps on the earth.' So, God created man in his own image, in the image of God he created him; male and female he created them." Genesis 2:18 reads, "And the Lord God said, it is not good that the man should be alone; I will make him a helper comparable to him." The primary purpose of marriage is to fellowship, have companionship, and help each other. In 2 Corinthians 6:14, Paul tells us, "Do not be unequally yoked together with unbelievers."

---

[2]   Meredith, Don and Sally, "Biblical Perspective on Marriage"

In "Biblical View of Marriage,"[3] Christopher Ash explains that marriage is a God-given voluntary, sexual, and public social union of one man and one woman, from different families, for the purpose of serving God.

What does the Bible say about marriage? Marriage was first instituted by God in the order of creation, given by God as an unchangeable foundation for human life. Marriage exists so that through it, humanity can serve God through children, through faithful intimacy, and through properly ordered sexual relationships. This union is patterned upon the union God has with His people, who are His bride, and the union Christ has with His church. Within marriage, husbands are to exercise a role of self-sacrificial headship, while wives are to posture godly submission to their husbands. This institution points us to our hope of Christ returning to claim His bride, making marriage a living picture of the gospel of grace.

Marriage shows us how deep and intimate our relationship with God can be. In honoring His design for marriage, we uphold the union of one man and one woman, united for life, with loving intimacy that reflects Christ that can bring new life into the world. God designed marriage to meet our need for companionship and to provide an illustration of our relationship with Him. The Bible says

---

[3] Ash, Christopher, "Biblical View of Marriage"

God comes first in our lives because He must be first. Everything else comes after Him. In Exodus 20:3, God says, "Thou shalt have no other gods before me." *Only* God can save you, your job, your children, and your spouse. God will give you direction for whatever you do in your life.

For premarital couples, it is so important to know God, for life is not complete without Him. God gives us leadership, guidance, and protection. Without Him, we would be lost. If Jesus had not died for us and shed His blood on the cross, there would be no remission of sins and we would be totally lost forever (1 Pet. 3:18). Thank God for Jesus!

Prior to marriage, choosing a partner who is equally yoked with you is a good ingredient for a relationship. If you are a believer and your partner is not, trouble will ensue. Being equally yoked means maintaining the same set of beliefs and values regardless of whether your parents raised you in church or not. If the two of you are not in one accord, you must seek God's guidance before you marry. God's love heals all things.

Beginning a relationship should also be based on transparency with each other, a practice that should last while you are married. Without transparency, trust becomes difficult. I know, sometimes there are some embarrassing moments in your lives that you prefer not to talk about, but to have a lasting marriage, you must have trust. Later in the book, I will present to you some important questions for beginning relationships.

God wants to save all of us, and He has a plan for us all. Nevertheless, the Bible says, "For God so loved the world that he gave his only begotten Son (Jesus Christ), that whoever believes in Him should not perish, but have everlasting life" (John 3:16). "For all have sinned and fall short of the glory of God" (Rom. 3:23). This means we all have a sinful nature and will make mistakes, but God is sovereign, all-knowing, and forgiving.

According to Carol Heffernan in "God's Design for Marriage"[4] as Christians, we know that applying biblical principles to our marriage will give us a stronger foundation than those of our unbelieving friends and neighbors. Everything in the Christian life flows from God's love for us. We start each day rejoicing in His love. When we love unconditionally, we are set free to love God and obey His Word. For so long, we have viewed His commands as restrictions on our lives, but we should begin to see them as loving reminders of what is good and not good for us. When we set God's love before our eyes, sin loses a lot of its temptation.

When God became the head of my life, I prayed for Him to send me that right person, and He answered my prayer. Today, I have an incredibly happy, peaceful, and loving marriage, equally

---

[4] Bible Info, "What Does the Bible Say About Marriage?"

yoked. Whenever you have doubt about your pre-marital partner, ask God to show you whether they are right for you, then just wait and be watchful. If they are not pleasing in His eyes, He will show you, but you must listen and pay attention.

Before my husband and I got married, we were very transparent about everything, and we continue to be while married. We truly trust one another. What keeps us grounded is prayer, studying God's Word, conversation, and commitment to a Bible-based church.

People will tell you marriage is hard work, omitting the fact that prayer changes things; I can attest to this. However, if you allow yourself to be grounded in the Word and continually focus on the Lord Jesus Christ with prayer and conversation with your spouse, I can almost guarantee marriage will not be hard work.

Stella and Merle's life together is an example of Genesis 2:18, in which God said, "It is not good for man to be alone. I will make a helper suitable for him." Here is an example of a marriage story that is good, caring, loving, and Christ-like, taken from the website "Our Daily Bread." In the article "Made For Each Other,"[5] Alyson Kieda shares about Stella and Merle, who have been happily married for seventy-nine years. Merle is now 101, and Stella is ninety-five. They are so close that neither is

---

[5] Hefferman, Carol, "God's Design for Marriage"

happy without the other. When Merle was recently admitted to a nursing home, he was miserable, so Stella decided to bring him back home. She needs a walker to get around on her own, but she has her grandchildren and wonderful neighbors to help her.

Similarly, Eve was the perfect companion for Adam, and through them, God instituted marriage. None of the creatures God brought before Adam fit the description of a companion, so He created Eve, made from the rib of Adam. She was Adam's suitable helper (Gen. 2:19-20). God's purpose of this marriage was not only the mutual aid of individuals; it was also to begin a family and to care for creation, which includes other people (Gen. 1:28). From that first family came a community so that, whether married or single, old or young, none of us would be alone. As a community, God has given us the privilege of sharing "each other's burdens" (Gal. 6:2).

According to Stuart Brisco in "God's Design for Marriage,"[6] the secret to a long marriage is to "keep your promises and live a long time." It is that simple and that fundamental. Marriage is as simple as ABC: "Adjustments Based on Commitments." Your foundation must be in place. God expects you to know four foundational principles to understand marriage. First, marriage is God's idea, not a creation of man, who thinks his intellect is in control. 1 Peter 4:8 says, "And above all things that have fervent love for one

---

[6] Kieda, Alyson, "Made for Each Other"

are a divine idea." Second, men and women are both made in the image of God. Gender and sexuality are His divine ideas, although there is a clear distinction between the two. Third, marriage requires sacrifice. The worst enemy in marriage is selfishness. When you are married, you must leave your single life behind. Fourth, marriage requires long-lasting commitment. If a marriage is not committed to "'til death do us part," it will be on shaky grounds and eventually fall. Two people should commit to the necessary adjustments to be able to handle all the various situations they will encounter in marriage. Through His Spirit, God takes a man and a woman in marriage and begins working in their lives, so they become one. They spend the rest of their days discovering what that oneness means. May God enable you to keep your promises and live a long time together.

Chapter Two

Questions to Ask before Marriage

*W*hen you first meet someone and you immediately feel that attraction and connection, you may think you are in love. Well, even though you might think it is love, it just may be infatuation. When you first meet someone, love and infatuation can look and feel similar. As I explained earlier, infatuation is short-term and love is long-lasting and continues to grow into a lifelong relationship. Therefore, the best way to approach a relationship is to become good friends first, and if your partner is willing, then it might be a good fit.

According to "10 Questions to Ask before Getting Married"[7] by Elizabeth Overstreet,[9] the best way to get your marriage off to a good start is to prepare some questions that you can ask your partner to get a better understanding of where you both stand before marriage.

---

[7] Brisco, Stuart, God's Design for Marriage"

- Find out what their religious beliefs are and if they attend church and how often. If both of you go to different churches, then a conversation needs to ensue. Without a spiritual background, marriage can be challenging.

- It would be helpful to know if your partner can display empathy for others, especially you. Think about it. What if you get sick? Will your partner be there for you?

- During stressful times and when frustration hits, it is vital to know how your partner handles these moments. Stress can be a relationship breaker, because some people do not handle stress very well.

- Find out if your partner is a passionate person. Being passionate is key, However, it is important to talk to one another, so learn more about each other's family and the relationship itself. Do you want children? If so, what are some of your values and beliefs in raising children?

- Where do you stand on intimacy? How often will intimacy play a part in your relationship?

- How would you handle a disagreement? Would you be willing to listen to one another before an argument gets out of hand?

- Who would handle the finances? Would either of you have transparency when it comes to finances?

- What if you fell out of love? How would you handle that? What are some things you can do to save your marriage? Consider making a pact that divorce is not an option.

Do you feel that getting married will make you whole by taking care of all your issues? If you do not feel whole while you are single, then you will not be whole when you get married. If you are not enough *without* your partner, you will never be enough *with* your partner. Only God has the recipe to make you whole (Phil. 4:19).

As I mentioned before, it is important to know if your partner is an unbeliever. If your partner is not a believer, he/she may want to do things socially that are out of alignment with the values of a believer, such as immorality, excessive drinking, or even drugs. This will be extremely uncomfortable for you. It is also important to know if your partner is equally yoked with you, because if there is no transparency with each other, the character, honesty, reliability, moral qualities, and personality will not be crystal clear. You see, if you do not find out these things up front, they will come out later after you are married. With that in mind, the good side of a person always comes out in the beginning. It is important to know what you want in a mate before you consider finding one. I cannot say this enough: transparency and communication are the key.

All this is important to keep from marrying for the wrong reasons and marrying the wrong person. That's why it is important to let God into your life, allowing Him to lead and guide you so you don't get caught up in satisfying words, such as "I love you," "You are so beautiful," "I'll do anything for you," "I want you," "I need you," etc. And do not forget about the materialistic things. Possessions will not make you happy in the long run. Ask your Lord and Savior to bring the right person into your life and to help you discern if that person is right for you. Isaiah 65:24 says, "'Before they call, I will answer; while they are still speaking, I will hear,' says the Lord."

Chapter Three

Adding the Right Ingredients
for a Healthy Marriage

I must tell you I now have a wonderful and God-fearing husband. He was very willing to tell his story as to how a husband should treat his wife. He came up with quite a few ways about how he treats his own wife. My husband believes a godly husband should pray and include God first in his life, as well as in all his thoughts.

Before I met my husband, I was alone and needed someone to talk with, go to the park with … just a male friend to enjoy life with. I prayed for God to send me a special godly man who loved Him before anything, someone who knew how to treat a woman, someone who knew how to give unconditional love—a husband who would be pleasing in God's eyes and compatible with me. These are all the right ingredients for a healthy marriage.

I decided to sign up for a matchmaking site with the hope of meeting that special someone. I talked with numerous guys who did not meet my qualifications. However, one day, this one guy appeared on the site. When I read his profile, the first thing I saw he wrote was "I Love God!" I said, "Bingo! This is the one!" So, we connected, and to my surprise, he had been praying, just as I did, to find that special partner to be in his life. We met, dated, and that is all she wrote. Six months later, we married.

God blessed me with the husband of my dreams. He answered my prayers, and He has surely given me a loving, peaceful marriage. This time around, divorce is not an option. Now, this marriage is all about God first. God gave me exactly what I asked for, and more. That is the beauty of prayer and asking Him for what we want from Him.

We live by Ephesians 5:25, which says, "For husbands, this means, love your wives, just as Christ loved the church." Also, 1 Corinthians 7:3-4 is important to us, which reads, "Let the husband render to his wife the affection due her, and likewise also the wife to her husband. The wife does not have authority over her own body, but the husband does, and likewise, the husband does not have authority over his own body, but the wife does."

When a couple mistreats each other by not giving the respect that is deserved, failing to listen to each other, and withholding the attention desired, that's when trouble begins. Then the marriage is a recipe for disaster. You might notice a change in the attitudes and actions from either partner.

A husband and wife should love one another with unconditional love, agape love. You see, there are many forms of love, and I will get into them a little later. My husband has a lot to say about how to treat a wife with agape love. He believes in being loving and kind, guarding her, protecting her, listening to her, and making her always feel respected.

My husband also speaks of a father's love for his children, that he should teach and train them in the way they should go. Always live life in a way that will honor God. Be transparent about everything with each other. Take the time to know your wife. Remember, "Happy wife, happy life." Compliment her often and tell her how beautiful she is; if you do not, someone else will. Do not get so complacent that you fail to take her out to dinner, surprise her with flowers or candy, or take her to a movie. These things are important in keeping your marriage together. Most importantly, get together and read God's Word. Live by the "golden rule," which is "Do unto others as you would have them to do unto you" (Matt. 7:12).

Let us talk love. The word "love" has many different meanings, and much of the time, it is used too loosely. By that, I mean it has no meaning.

In "Hide and Seek,"[8] Neel Burton, MD, writes about the seven different styles of love:

Agape Love is love that is unconditional—a love that does not change no matter the situation. This is the kind of love God has for us. The Bible tells us God's unconditional love never fails and is not motivated by personal gain. No matter what happens in your marriage, you should be there for your wife or husband unconditionally. I can honestly say my husband and I have agape love for one another (1 Pet. 4:8).

Eros love is a sexual or passionate love. It can also be considered a romantic love. However, this type of love is usually expressed during physical intimacy between a husband and wife. Read Song of Solomon 1:2-4 for more teaching on eros love.

Philia Love is an affectionate or authentic love or friendship, such as a love between a father and his son or an elder and a younger. The relationships involved in philia make this type of love symmetrical.

Philautia Love is self-love. You must love yourself before you can have brotherly love. Love is patient, love is kind; it does not envy, it does not boast; it is not proud. It is rude, it is not self-seeking, it is not easily angered, it keeps no count of wrongs. Charity suffereth long. And is kind; charity envieth

---

[8] Overstreet, Elizabeth, "10 Questions to Ask Before Getting Married"

not; charity vaunteth not itself, is not puffed up, (1 Cor. 13:4)

Storge Love is a familiar love. This love is natural or instinctive, such as the love a mother has for her child.

Pragma Love is enduring love. This kind of love values practical aspects of a relationship as the most important and driving force. The pragmatic lover weighs up what they consider to be important traits for their relationship and their partner.

Ludus Love is playful love. Usually, this love is an uncommitted love; a person with this kind of love often lies a lot and does not stay committed in a relationship.

Manic Love is obsessive love. This love can be possessive, and it exhibits extreme jealousy, which can involve stalking. It can seem to make a person act crazy and dangerous.

When God is a part of your life, you should pray and ask Him for help to direct your marriage in the way it should go. This is vital because you cannot manage a marriage all by yourself, especially when you do not know where to begin. When things start falling apart, believe that when you let God in, He will be there for you. Everything you do should involve God, especially in your marriage. God is the only one who can work things out for you, so do not be afraid to go to Him for anything. "Do not lean to your own understanding" (Pr. 3:5-6).

According to The Knot's article, "Wedding,"[9] couples who wish to show their devotion to each other and their faith often turn to Bible verses about marriage when planning their nuptials. For couples who are lives are grounded in faith, planning a wedding is not only about planning for a life together, It's also about planning for a lifetime of worship and spiritual devotion as one.

Marriage Creed "Love Never Fails"[10] shares a creed of ten excellent marriage actions that couples should do in love during their marriage.

Comfort each other. Provide a refuge and sanctuary for your spouse.

Caress as you would be caressed. Warm your loved one's body with your healing touch.

Be a friend and a partner. In a world of turmoil and strife, friendship can be a peaceful island, separate and apart.

Be open with each other. Do not bind yourself in secret, for this causes suspicion and doubt.

---

[9] Burton, Neel, "Hide and Seek"

[10] The Knots Article, "Wedding | Wedding Planning Website Inspiration"

Listen to each other. Hear your spouse's words, as well as their non-language of tone, mood, and expression.

Respect each other. Each person is entitled to their own choices and mistakes in a marriage

Allow the other to be an individual. Do unto others as you would want done unto you.

Give each other approval. Do not criticize, but compliment.

Cherish the union. Let no one come between your togetherness—not your child, or friend.

Love one another. Love is your river of life above all else. Therefore, love one another.

"Marriage Poem"[11]–By Odessa Best

This poem was given to me from Odessa Best, 2017, a loving Christian friend who perished in a tragic car accident and is solely missed.

M – Meet each other's needs as often as possible.

---

[11] Best, Odessa, "Marriage Poem"

A – Ask God to change you and do not try to change your spouse.

R – Rest in the Lord and trust Him.

R – Rule out bitterness and resentment. Instead, develop a forgiving spirit.

I – Ignore petty issues and gossip.

A –Ask God for faith to remain faithful to your commitment to each other.

G –Grow in Christ Jesus daily. Give your life totally to God.

E–Erase the pain and suffering that you have caused each other in the past.

Chapter Four

Recipe for a Godly Marriage

Ingredients from "The Great Family Cookbook Project"[12]

Walk in sacrificial love...Ephesians 5:25 – "Husbands, love your wives, just as Christ also loved the church and gave Himself for her."

Avoid all immorality, impurity, and evil talk... Hebrews 13:4 – "Marriage is honorable among all, and the bed undefiled; but fornicators and adulterers God will judge."

Walk in the light...Psalm 89:15 – "Blessed are the people who know the joyful Sound. They walk, O Lord, in the light of Your countenance."

Learn what pleases the Lord...Hebrews 11:6 – "But without faith it's impossible to please Him,

---

[12] Marriage Creed, "Love Never Fails"

for he who comes to God must believe that He is, and that He is a rewarder of those who diligently seek Him."

Expose unfruitful deeds of darkness...Ephesians 5:11 – "And have no fellowship with the unfruitful works of darkness, but rather expose them."

Walk wisely and not unwisely...Ephesians 5:15 – "See then that you walk circumspectly, not as fools but as wise, redeeming the time, because the days are evil."

Be filled with the Holy Spirit...1 Corinthians 12:13 –"For by one Spirit we were all baptized into one body—whether Jews or Greeks, whether slaves or free—and have all been made to drink into one Spirit."

Make melody with your heart to the Lord... Ephesians 5:19 – "Speaking to one another in psalms and hymns and spiritual songs, singing and making melody in your heart to the Lord."

Do not be foolish and understand God's will...1 Thessalonians 5:18 – "In everything give thanks; for this is the will of God in Christ Jesus for you."

Be subject to one another in Christ… Ephesians 5:21 – "Submitting to one another for the fear of God."

Wives be subject to and respect your husband…Ephesians 5:22-23 –"Wives, submit to your own husbands as to the Lord. For the husband is head of the wife, as also Christ is head of the church; and He is the Savior of the body."

Husbands love your wives as Christ loved the Church…Ephesians 5:25-26 – "Husbands, love your wives just as Christ also loved the church and gave Himself for her that He might sanctify and cleanse her with the washing of water by the word."

Be holy and blameless by the washing of the word of God…Colossians 3:16 – "Let the word of Christ dwell in you richly in all wisdom, teaching and admonishing one another in psalms and hymns and spiritual songs, singing with grace in your hearts to the Lord."

Directions: Make sure all ingredients are used in full. No substitutions.

Mix well and add all the above to the marriage. Start immediately and wait patiently.

Notes: Time will make the marriage even better than it was at the beginning. Always rely on the

Lord's strength. The two of you will be blessed beyond measure (Based on Eph. 5:1-33).

Ellen G. White, in "Testimonies Relative to Marriage Duties,"[13] shares that no person professing to be a Christian should enter a marriage relationship until the husband is able to sustain the wife and the family. This is vital to see if God can be glorified by the union. Then the person should duly consider the result of every privilege of the marriage relationship, and the sanctified principle should be the basis of every action. In the increase of the person's family, he/she should take into consideration whether God would be glorified or dishonored by the couple bringing children into the world. Both the husband and wife should seek to glorify God at their first union, as well as during every year of their married life. They should consider what provision can be made for their children. They have no right to bring children into the world to be a burden to others.

---

[13] Walking Free: Recipe for a Godly Marriage, "The Great Family Cookbook Project"

Chapter Five

The Role of the Wife in Marriage

According to Dennis and Barbara Rainey in "Family Life,"[14] both husband and wife have a specific role in a marriage. First, I would like to begin with the role of the wife, followed by the role of the husband. When God made a man, He realized that man should not be alone, so He put Adam to sleep and removed one of his ribs, which He used to make a woman whom He called Eve (Gen. 2:22). Therefore, the role of the woman is to help her husband, and God expects this of the wife.

God wants you to respect your husband (Eph. 5:33). Respecting your husband means to have a deep admiration for him in all his abilities, qualities, and achievements. Also, regard his feelings, listen to him, and be a companion to him. Show respect by the way you treat him and think about him, always be polite and kind, let him know he matters, and avoid taking him for granted by thanking him when he

---

[14] White, Ellen G., Testimonies Relative to Marriage Duties"

does something for you. Moreover, having respect means you accept your husband for who he is even if you disagree with him. When you have respect in your relationship, you will build feelings of trust and safety together.

Love your husband by being committed to him through fulfilling his needs. Just as Christ is the head of the church, your husband is the head of the house. You must submit to your husband as the Bible teaches (Eph. 5:22-23). Submitting to your husband only means that as a wife, you must make a choice to not overtly resist your husband's will. Wait…this does not mean you cannot disagree or express your opinion; it just means you must accept the fact that your husband is the head of the household and, subsequently, honor what God has put in place.

All these characteristics fit together like baking a delicious pound cake. When a pound cake is mixed and baked, it comes out smooth, firm, and good. When it comes out of the oven, you have a beautifully baked cake, ready to serve. This is like how your marriage should be—trouble-free, solid, and ethical, so it will glorify God. A wife should know herself, know trust, and know forgiveness. Then God will be pleased.

Communication is the key to marriage. A wife should be a supportive best friend to her husband and listen to him. It takes teamwork to make a marriage, and it requires both partners to put in their individual efforts to make things work.

Sister Mercades Mitchell's testimony on the role of a wife.

The first wife in the human family was Eve. God Himself provided her for Adam, and God Himself performed the first marriage ceremony. Genesis 2:18 says, "And the Lord God said, 'it is not good that man should be alone; I will make him a helper comparable to him' (a helper corresponding to him, one who was fitted to be his companion)." After the ceremony, Adam said, "This is now bone of my bone and flesh of my flesh" (Gen. 2:23). God does not want us to be disconnected, isolated, and without social support, hence the family.

So, a true marriage is a union of three: God, husband, and wife. The recognition of this truth is the beginning of a healthy recipe for marriage. God should be at the marriage and throughout the marriage. The wife is an integral part of the family unit. A wife who is converted and has surrendered her life to God will get divine wisdom and instruction from her daily walk with God as to how to fulfil this especially important role.

The Lover: A wife will love her husband. True love is precious. It is a high and holy principle. It is a plant of heavenly growth, and it must be fostered and nourished. Love is power. Love is of God. Love will gain victory when argument and authority are powerless. It is diffusive in its nature and quiet in its operation, yet strong and mighty in its purpose to overcome great evils. It is deep and abiding; it is not a selfish passion. It bears fruit, and it will lead a wife to a constant effort to make her husband happy. It is unselfish; it seeks not its own. It is patient and long-suffering. Its definition is clearly out-lined in 1 Corinthians 13.

The Friend: A wife will be a friend to her husband. Marriage should be based on true friendship, and husbands and wives should treat each other with tact, courtesy, and respect. A happy married life is impossible without these ingredients. Wives study your husband and familiarize yourself with his needs. Every man has disagreeable traits or what you consider disagreeable. For example, he may forget to put the cap on the toothpaste after use. Understand that you cannot transform your husband; adapt and do the best to avoid wounding his self-respect by nagging and criticizing. Learn his unsuspected weaknesses and defects but focus on the strengths. Let there be mutual love and mutual forbearance.

Respect is especially important to a man. A wife's commitment to the relationship with her husband will make her think first and foremost of her husband's well-being. She will not provoke an inferiority complex in her husband by criticizing him, especially in the presence of the children and in public. Ephesians 4:26 says, "Be ye angry and sin not; let not the sun go down on your wrath." It is important to understand that a wife can be angry without being disrespectful and rude. It is always a precious thing to hear, "I am sorry," if this principle is violated. Ephesians 4:5 says, "Be ye kind to one another, tenderhearted, forgiving one another, even as God for Christ's sake hath forgiven you."

Around every family there is a sacred circle that should be kept unbroken. No other has any right in that sacred circle. "The heart of the wife should be the grave of the faults of the husband," says Ellen White in the book **The Adventist Home**.[15] She should not permit another person to share the confidences that belong solely to themselves. Never should either party (husband or wife) indulge in a joke at the expense of the other's feelings. Proverb 31:11 says, "She openeth her mouth with wisdom and in her tongue is the law of kindness, the heart of her husband doth safely trust in her." Verse 12 says, "She will do him good and not evil all the days of her life."

Homemaker: A wife cannot make her home agreeable and happy unless she possesses a love for order, preserves her dignity, and has good government. She knows how to live within her means and avoid excesses and extravagance without being "stingy." She should understand nutrition and the culinary arts and should know how to present simple foods in its most attractive form, thus contributing to the health of the husband and family. Body and spirit are often restored at the family table. They say the home is the man's castle and a considerate wife will endeavor to make the home a place where his "heart is."

---

[15] Rainey, Dennis and Barbara, "Family Life"

The Christian: It is important that wives remain interesting and attractive to their husbands over the years. When a woman is attractive to a man it is more than physical beauty. While it is important to take pride in her appearance so that her husband will be proud of her and not apologetic about her presence, beauty is more than skin-deep. Proverbs 31:30 says, "Favor is deceitful, and beauty is vain but a woman that feareth the Lord, she shall be praised." It is a godly character that makes a woman beautiful. The husband will continue to be grateful that "whoso findeth a wife findeth a good thing" (Pr. 18:22).

Daily family worship that includes Bible reading and family prayer is indispensable and is a wall that protects the home against many dangers. It prepares the family to meet the challenges, perplexities, discouragements, and disappointments that will come. Indeed, "the family that prays together stays together."

The role of a wife can be challenging, but it is rewarding. When God is in the marriage, the result of the years together, in the words of Ellen White, is not a "tissue fabric, but a texture that has borne the wear and tear and test and trial of time"[16] But hearts will still be bound together in the golden bonds of a love that is enduring.

---

[16] White, Ellen G., ***The Adventist Home***

Chapter Six

The Role of the Husband in Marriage

These qualities of God have designed a perfect recipe that, when husbands and wives follow it, will create just the marriage God intended. According to "What Should Be the Husband's Role in Marriage,"[17] Dennis Rainey explains that there are "Biblical Responsibilities for the Husband." First, a husband needs to be the leader of his household. In the Scriptures, God has made the role of the husband clear. "Christ is the head of every man, and the man is the head of the woman, and God is the head of Christ" (1 Cor. 11:3).

The most important qualities of a good husband include the ability to be a God-fearing person who obeys God's commandments, independent, and a good leader. Wives want their husbands to be affectionate by being sweet and romantic as well as loyal and trustworthy. The husband must love himself to

---

[17] White, Ellen G., *Mind, Character & Personality*, "tissue fabric, but a texture that has borne…

love his wife. A husband should be truthful, honest, and transparent. A good husband should also be self-disciplined and know how to control himself. Wives expect their husbands to understand them and know their wants and needs. It is so important to be faithful in a marriage, for unfaithfulness will cause unhappiness and possible breakup of the marriage. It is also particularly important for a husband to be forgiving, to not look back on past mistakes or become vengeful.

To live a happy life with his wife, his children, and himself, a husband must know how to forgive, forget, and move forward.

This good husband I have mentioned is not easy to find among some men. However, if a man is truly in love—and I mean, he has unconditional love, better known as agape love—he will strive to develop those qualities. A husband should cherish his wife above everyone else. Aside from God, the wife should be the most important person in a husband's life, and this relationship should be based on deep, personal love for each other. Ephesians 5:25 says a husband should love his wife the way Christ loved the church. When founded upon good qualities, a healthy marriage will balance out the faults of both the husband and the wife.

This is my husband Larry's testimonial story on the role of a husband in a marriage.

On my way home from work, one hot July afternoon, I saw this gorgeous lady and three other ladies sitting on the porch, taking a break from work. One of the ladies was my BFF (best female friend). So, after I got home later that evening, I paid my BFF a visit to inquire as to the identity of the beautiful lady she was sitting with on the porch. She asked if I was interested in her. Of course, I said yes. The following afternoon, my friend called me with a name and telephone number.

Later that evening, I called her. When she answered, she had the sweetest voice I had ever heard. When we met later that evening, she informed me she was twenty-two years old. I was twenty-one. She had three sons. They ranged from the ages six months to fifteen months to seven years old. That night, we talked for hours, just getting to know each other. I was nearly late for work the next morning. On my part, it was love at first sight. From that point forward, we were inseparable, except when I had to deploy overseas. I was in the United States Air Force. We were married September 1971, and a little more than a month later, we lost our baby son. He was nine months old when he died.

We were married for forty-six years. Both of us had health challenges and money problems. She had serious trust issues from previous relationships. We had great communication; we were a team and very much in love. I had to work super hard to gain her complete trust.

June 3, 1981, I had a near-fatal fall through the roof of a tall building, with a large motor sitting on my shoulder. That was when Christ started to enter my life and marriage. It was a miracle I survived. That was one of many miracles He performed in my life and marriage.

Shortly after I retired in 2012, my wife became gravely ill and was placed on life support and in a coma for six days. I prayed long and hard. God answered my prayers. After a month, it was suggested that I put her into a long-term healthcare facility. I refused and took her home. I was her primary caregiver for seven years. She was back in the hospital one month before she passed in 2017.

Just before she passed, I was in terrible condition, both mentally and physically, so much until my two daughters suggested I needed a friend to go fishing with, to have lunch with, and/or just someone to talk with. I was very overweight, depressed, and nearly exhausted. I walked with a cane and a walker. I prayed to God, feeling that I had a short time to live. I asked God to please allow me a little bit of the fruits of my labor. All my adult life, I worked hard and several jobs to provide for my wife and children. Along the way, with God's guidance and reading His Word, I learned His requirements for being a good Christian husband and father.

To show how God works, after my first wife passed, I had been on several dating sites looking for a friend/Christian companion to talk to, have dinner with, etc. Just as I had decided to give up, a beautiful lady appeared. I read her profile; she was explicit in her requirements for a man. She was all about God. My thought was that she *must be holier than thou; lol, but we were on the same page. She called; we talked. We agreed to meet, and as they say, the rest is history.*

For the start, both of us were Christians; we put God first in our lives and decisions. We prayed and asked God for His guidance. We communicate very well; we have mutual respect. We do a lot of things together; we are best friends as well as lovers. We make all major decisions together. We make it a practice never to go to bed angry. They say marriage is a 50/50 partnership, but that is not necessarily true; both parties must be committed to whatever it takes for their relationship to succeed.

When we were dating, my wife and I were of different religious denominations. When I proposed, we discussed which church to attend. She decided she would give up her Church and be baptized into my faith. We are now married and have been for nearly three years. I leave these thoughts with you. If you want to be happy for the rest of your life, put God first. The following Scripture references will be a great help: 1 Peter 4; Colossians 3; 1 Corinthians 16. God's recipes for marriage.

Chapter Seven

Testimonies

Sister Valerie Dyson gave her testimony on marriage as a Pastor's Wife

If anyone thinks that marriage is going to be a walk in the park or that it is 50/50, it is not true, because we come with different issues, situations, and backgrounds and we think differently. That is just the nature of it. My husband and I have been married for forty-three years as of June 2020. We are truly as different as night and day; for example, I like containers of butter and he likes sticks of butter, but to me they are messy and unattractive. We like what we like, right? I will put the butter in a decorative container, so we compromise to make it work, because after all, we are human. I would describe our life together as being on a roller coaster ride.

I am a pastor's wife, and I have been through a lot. What people do not realize is we are just like them, but we are held to a higher standard in their eyes, and to be honest, we should be. But we all make mistakes

in life, and we can make a wrong turn. When my husband first told me he wanted to go to school to be a minister, I was like, "No, no way." I never wanted to be a doctor, lawyer, or pastor's wife, because I knew those jobs would require him to be away from the family, more so than someone with a nine-to-five job. My husband and I have separated, divorced, and then remarried again. We had a big wedding and all with our family, church family, and friends in attendance. I know you probably wonder what happened. Well, for me, I felt he was more dedicated to the church and its members than to me. There was also a lack of communication, which is key in a happy and successful marriage. When the divorce was finalized, it took two years. Oddly enough, I really did not feel like we were divorced. Our daughter was away serving in the Air Force. Our sons were teenagers at the time, my older son wanted to be with his dad, and our youngest was with me. As time went on, we would talk, and we listened to each other. I made it truly clear that God comes first and then family; everything else comes after that. 1 Corinthians 7:10 says, "And unto the married I command, yet not all, but the Lord, let not the wife depart from her husband." God has given us such good instructions from the B-I-B-L-E. It is all in there.

2019 was the hardest year of our lives. Divorce and separation were nothing compared to the loss of our youngest son, Maurice, who was thirty-seven at the time and fell ill in a matter of days. He passed away on Mother's Day. I cannot explain that hurt and void *you feel. This was going to make or break us. We were so close to calling it quits for good, but God stepped in and miraculously showed us the best gift we could possibly give to each other and our son: to love each other that much more, which is what we have done. It is like starting all over again with a newfound love. I do not live as someone with no hope. Thessalonians 4:16 says, "For the Lord himself shall descend from heaven with a shout, with the voice of the archangel, and with the trump of God: and the dead in Christ shall rise first." Because of that passage of Scripture, I knew we would see our beautiful son again.*

If I can say anything to you in making your marriage work, remember that communication is the key. Through it all, be kind and respectful to each other with Jesus. It will take you a long way. And the church said amen. Be blessed.

The following is the testimony of **Sister Dorothy Jackson's marriage**

Growing up, you see and hear of marriages full of life and love. I am sure these marriages had some rocky and challenging days, but through it all, they learned to depend upon the Lord. Then you wonder what made them get married in the first place…was its wealth, kindness, or friendship? I think the songwriter, Michael Bolton, said it best when he said, "When a man loves a woman, she can do no wrong." My husband and I felt a connection between us when we first met. I was blown away by his kindness, his compassion, and his gentleman-like character. He opened doors for me. We would sit for hours just enjoying time with each other. We would talk about nothing for hours, and before we knew it, it was time to leave. I genuinely believe God had a plan for the two of us to get married. Being married to my husband has given me stability, happiness, love, and most of all, spiritual companionship.

After thirty-eight years of marriage, with the help of the Lord, my husband is still the breadwinner. He continues to make me happy, shows me kindness, and is full of compassion. He still opens doors for me. We continue to talk about any and everything for hours, just enjoying time with each other. Most of all, we both love each other very, very much, and for that we give God the glory for the unity of our marriage. I try to treat him like a king, and he treats me like a queen. Loving your spouse is not about what your spouse does for you; it is about what you do for them.

Elder Glen Mitchell shares his marriage testimony below.

The role of a husband in marriage is to be head of the household. God put man in charge of the union. Most women are seeking a man (a husband) who is strong and who takes the lead in the marriage. A godly, ordained marriage is a union between a man and a woman. Decisions should be made jointly; however, the husband should be a strong decision maker. The husband should love and respect his wife. Although Ephesians 5:22 says that "wives should submit to their own husbands as to the Lord," Ephesians 5:25 says, "Husband, love your wives, even as Christ also loved the church, and gave himself for it." The husband should be a role model for the children and teach the boys how to grow into productive, God-fearing men. God intended for the family to be made up of a man and a woman. This dynamic makes for a wholesome family. The husband should model to his sons how a man should treat a woman, and to his daughters what they should expect from a man, and nothing less.

July 27 of this year will be my thirty-third year of marriage to my wife. I thank God for His guidance and for blessing me with a godly wife. A good husband is a God-fearing man. He should welcome the partnership of his wife. God formed a woman from the rib of a man, meaning that she should walk by his side and not behind. A good husband should support the growth of his wife. He should lead out in family worship, and not just take his family to church but attend church with them. The greatest God that children may ever see is the God they see in their father and mother. As women are more emotional beings than men, to foster an emotionally intelligent marriage, the husband should pay attention to his wife, seeking to know and discern what she is feeling. Through this, he will make an emotional connection with her. A godly husband is to protect his wife with his own life, physically, emotionally, and above all else, spiritually.

Elder Jimmie Bynum's marriage testimony.

Before I got married, I prayerfully asked the Lord to send me a dedicated Christian wife—someone who loves Him and who has committed her life to His service. The Lord heard and miraculously answered my prayers by allowing me to meet a wonderful Christian young lady. Quickly after meeting her, I knew she loved the Lord and that she was totally committed to following Christ. Spending time together and with Christ, we grew to love each other.

After a dating period of about two years, we got married, and we have been married for twenty-three years. The Lord has tremendously blessed our marriage. One of the things I loved early in the marriage was finally having a mate who enjoyed sharing the Christian walk with me. Some of our happiest times together are on Sabbath when we are together in Sabbath school and church service. We find great fulfillment sharing the message of salvation in the prisons, in nursing homes, and to the sick and shut in.

We believe the success of a Christian marriage is to have the Lord as the center of the marriage. Every day, we religiously have family worship, spending time together to study God's Word and to pray together for others. As the Lord works daily in our individual lives, He also works in our marriage, drawing us together as one. Truly the family that prays together stays together.

Daily life is filled with challenges, seen and unseen, but having Jesus at the center of our marriage, we do not meet these challenges alone. Whatever the challenges may be—financial issues, work issues, behavioral issues, physical issues—with God at the center of the marriage, He can resolve all issues, whether physical or spiritual.

The Bible says in Ephesians 4:26, "Be ye angry, and sin not; let not the sun go down upon your wrath." In our marriage, the Lord has enabled us to practice this text, and in twenty-three years of marriage, we have never gone to bed mad at each other. As a husband, I can safely say I have never had to sleep in the dog-house, and I thank God for that. I have a wife who understands that no one is perfect and who is willing to forgive and move on. She often says everybody comes to a marriage with baggage, some with a couple bags while some come with a U-Haul, so we must be willing to forgive each other.

My wife is a good homemaker and a woman who believes the Lord gave man the responsibility to be the priest in the home. In her love for the Lord, she gives to me the respect God requires a wife to give to her husband, and I give to her the love God requires of me. In 1 Timothy 5:8, the Bible says, "But if any provide not for his own, and especially for those of his own house, he has denied the faith, and is worse than an Infidel."

I believe and practice this text, and with the partner-ship with my wife, together we have provided for our own. We supported two children through college who both received bachelor's degrees debt-free. They both went on to graduate school to complete master's degrees and are living successful lives, thanks to God. Together we have also helped deserving college students, both local and international, with financial support while they are in college. Helping others who are in need, as the Lord directs, gives a joy that cannot be explained.

The Lord has blessed us in more ways than we can explain, and we thank Him for being the glue in our marriage that has kept it together.

Sister Donnell Powell shares her testimony of a roller coaster marriage.

My marriage journey was forty years, but it was not what I signed up for. God walked and talked with me during my career, child rearing, and my marriage, with its ups and downs, including counseling, separation, divorce filing, divorce dissolution, confession, forgiveness, reconciliation, anointing, and the death of my spouse.

No one could have told me in the beginning days that I would not have a near-perfect marriage. All the right boxes were checked, as I exclaimed to my first cousin, "I am going to have a happy marriage, or I am going to die trying." This was my honest belief. My sister later said, "The enemy was listening to you, and he started his hellish work to destroy your marriage, your mate, you, and your children." Forty years later, battle-scarred and worn, on the brink of divorce, I petitioned God with these words: "Lord, please don't let me drink this bitter cup."

I had three adult children, all married with children of their own, who were devastated and in disbelief that their sixty-three-year-old parents were in the throes of a divorce. Their parents who had looked out for their every need and taught them Christian principles on which they had established their families. Their parents who had educated them in the schools of the prophets, paid their tuition so they had no college loans, attended their graduations, participated in their weddings, assisted them in purchasing their first home, and were there for the birth of each grandchild…now on the brink of divorce. How could it be?

I had to be open with them, tell them the plain truth, solicit their prayers for their father, while not destroying their concepts and experience of who he was as a father to them. I let them know who he was as a father was different from who he was as a husband. I told them they were free to ask questions, state their feelings, and enter the conversation on any level they wanted to. As a family of five, we communicated by group emails that we could all read. They spoke up and did not hold back.

To make a long story short, I filed for a divorce, retired, and moved out of state. I lived with a friend who traveled out of state weekly, giving me space and time to pray, communicate, and avail myself of not only legal counsel, but personal professional counsel as well. It also gave me time to set goals, to grow as a person, and to find a measure of peace in what were beautiful surroundings.

After eighteen months, God in His wisdom and mercy directed me back at the request of my husband, who had been diagnosed with bone cancer.

God was not through with me yet, as He opened portals of prayer, confession, forgiveness, reconciliation, anointing, caregiving, death, and salvation. This not only included my husband and me, but each of our children and their spouses. My son preached his dad's funeral. We buried him in his hometown in the family and community cemetery.

God had set us free. My husband was set free in death, and now he awaits the call of the life giver. My children and I were set free in life to live our lives, choosing to focus on the good memories and looking forward to reuniting with my husband and their day in the earth made new, where he will be a perfect being and we will as well, by the grace and mercy of God.

This is my story. Not everyone would have lived it my way, but I honestly have few regrets.

Nadine Clipper, whose single dating life was up and down.

I would like to dedicate this narrative to my dear friend, Marion Oates, as an act of love. She is granted permission to include some, all, or none of the information shared. The experiences are true; however, the names of the characters have been changed for the purpose of this writing. It is my deepest pleasure to reflect and write what has been going on with me in the dating world. My journey has been twofold: dating as a secular woman and then as a woman of God.

The Bible instructs us in Matthew 6:33, "But seek first the kingdom of God and His righteousness, and all these things shall be added to you." At this crossroad, I had a life-changing decision to make; I could continue selecting the profiles of guys I was encountering, or I could allow God to be the head of my life. This commitment to God includes all areas that exist and concern me.

The profiles of some of the selected men included men who were emotionally, financially, and sometimes physically unavailable, due to their personal life choices. Yet, I found myself attracting and, in principle, participating in practices that contradicted the values I convinced myself I was using as a guide while engaging with men.

I was not honoring my values of trust, honesty, chastity, active spiritual life practice, financial security, vision, goals, and a plan of action to achieve purpose. I oftentimes violated my own boundaries. It was apparent I needed an inner revival to identify and heal the wounds that were still bleeding. I managed to cover up the wounds from my childhood that still needed to be unpacked and restored. Surely, all the previous therapeutic work healed this and that already, and I should be ready for the love of a lifetime, right?

My inner transformation became a part of my everyday living after I sat in my mess, unpacked my secrets with God through confession, and sought His presence in my life. Still to this day, journaling helps with the inner dialogue I have with myself. I call my inner voices my "Board Members." They include God's voice; the voice of negativity—in essence, the enemy— the voices of other people telling us this or that; ego, etc. Laugh if you want...I know you have "Board Members" too because we all do.

As I continue to ground down in God's Word with daily reading, praying, and quiet time, I put on the armor of God (Eph. 6:11) and strive to thrive as a Proverbs 31 woman, which is like rubies...who can find her?

We all have a past, present, and future. I am spilling the tea regarding my dating journey as a fifty-four-year-old queen with commendable secular credentials. I have also been single and celibate for several years now as well.

I have learned that the dating scene is a whole lot different than it used to be ten to twenty years ago. I remember times of courting a gentleman who would be interested, as he would get to know you as a human *being—not so much these days. Now, I have come across men, or men have crossed my path, who seem to only want to text and talk shallow words, then have sex. So, let us talk about the texting piece first. The conversations are so surface level...what do I mean by that? Generally, I have found that over a different caliber of men, many speak in one-word conversations and acronyms like "WYD," for example. I often text back for clarification, and I assault my assumptions before I provide a response. For some people, the acronym "WYD" means "What you are doing?" For others, it might mean something else.*

For the purpose of this writing, I want to provide a real-life experience I had with a man I met online, who happened to work in the same building in which I work but in different departments. The information below is true to the best of my recollection.

God, thank You for protecting me from the liars and cheaters. Thank You for guiding my path and teaching me the lessons I must learn on this journey. Thank You for sharpening my intuition and faith. Thanks for insight and analytics to connect the dots in this experience.

As we move forward, and our paths cross, please shine in and through me. Teach me to show loving kindness, despite a man's intentions.

Amen...
Nadine

Chapter Eight

Principal Ingredients to Stay Married

In **"4 Vital Ingredients for Staying Married,"**[18] Andrew Linder shares ingredients that are important to remain married "'til death do us part." ***They are love, trust, transparency, and prayer***. The first and most important ingredient for marriage is a commitment to ***love,*** which is the basis for keeping a marriage together. When you first get married, you feel you are in love, yet eventually, you truly fall in unconditional love. However, if you fail to commit to unconditional love, there is a chance that problems can occur and uncouple the relationship. Sometimes love does not win in the end. Other issues such as selfishness, pride, anger, and broken trust might win instead. So, when you commit to a lifelong love, you will find it will be the most powerful force in your marriage. It will be enduring, sacrificial, and unconditional.

---

[18] Rainey, Dennis, "Biblical Responsibilities for The Husband"

To make sure your marriage continues to thrive, you must have **trust** and **transparency.** It is important to communicate with each other, no matter what issues arise. Communication helps you and your spouse get to know each other intimately, physically, and spiritually. Communication is the key.

Most importantly, to stay married, you must keep God in your life. Develop a plan to **pray** together, study your Bible with one another, and make sure you attend a Bible-based church to maintain an ongoing spirituality toward each other and God. Marriage is a covenant between God, husband, and wife. If you want your marriage to truly succeed, you should place an emphasis on spirituality.

Marriage is designed to be desirable and enjoyable. It should be **fun**. Keep your marriage on a continual honeymoon. Remember the way it was when you first met and became newlyweds; you went on getaways, you both flirted with each other, you couldn't stay away from each other, you gave and received flowers, and you both complimented each other. All the things you did before the marriage should continue in new and different ways as you pursue your marriage. Therefore, keeping variety, adventure, spontaneity, play, and laughter in your marriage is so important. Your marriage should never die; keep it interesting.

Mary Thomas, who had three failed marriages.

All of us believed fairy tales were true because our parents told us they were, such as Santa Claus, the tooth fairy, Easter and the egg, etc. Well, to break our bubble in early adolescence, we found out these were factious lies, more diplomatically speaking, tales told to all juveniles which have been carried down from generation to generation. In due time, we realized the tales are fabrications. Hello, world! "Life is not a bowl of cherries."

I have said this to say—and maybe you have guessed where I am coming from—my life was not anything like those fairy tales I was told. All my marriages, three to be exact—especially the last—were something I would not wish on my enemies, not that I have any, but just as a matter of speaking.

Before I begin telling you about my life with my third husband, I want to speak to newlyweds or potential prospects. Listen up. Please do not think all outcomes are the same. It is a matter of how you go about it. Please, please love the person to whom you are going to say, "I do." Love the Lord your God with all your heart, and your mate should be of the same accord.

This is the one and only way for matrimony because love is the key for living. Yes, this is my problem, as you will learn from me; it was my mistake in the beginning. I did love the Lord from childhood. I was raised in the Catholic church, went to Catholic schools, married my second husband in the Catholic faith, and raised his twins in the Catholic faith and schools. So, I knew the Lord and His goodness. Any religious denomination can give you this by studying His Word and following His commandments. But I guess my faith had failed. Maybe, I do not know. I began taking measures in my own hands, doing it my way instead of seeking the Lord and following His guidance. My downfall was marrying for security and not for love.

During my third marriage, I married a man who was "streetwise," a person who knew all the angles in life. He was a great carpenter. Our home was beautiful. He was very generous with his money to me and to my family. I felt security for me and my children. But here is the kicker: he did not know how to romance me; he did not show love behind closed doors, only in public places and around people he deceived. He was a liar, a cheater, and all that comes with it. He was not a comforter. I kept my strength up by working, going to church, and being with my children. His devotion to the Lord was only on New Year's Eve. He had many faults, which I kept secret for many, many years and coped with all of them until all my children were grown and married. He grew up in a home that did not show love. He did not have a role model in his life. He had a good job and worked away from home on the railroad for weeks at a time. He seldom called me . My home life behind closed doors with him was miserable. I felt lonely when I was home. I wanted the fairy tale I had grown to believe in as a child to come true. I needed to believe in myself. I *needed the Lord I had given up, thinking I could do it on my own. I thought I needed the tangible way to feel and see it happening. All my worries mounted and mounted. I had two strokes, one in 2009, when I fell out on my job and never went back. I decided to retire after working for forty-five years at the same place. The second stroke was in 2013. All through this, the Lord kept me. I did not have any residual effects after both attacks. I had to go through these hardships to find out the Lord never left me even though I had forsaken Him. He was right there, holding me in His arms, comforting me, and He had true love for me all the time. I asked the Lord for His forgiveness. Praise God. He is good and worthy of all the praise.*

Chapter Nine

Growing Your Faith in God

Parker, Ken and Kay, "The ABC's of Becoming a Christian."[19] To grow in Christ, three essentials are a must. They are the ABC's for Christian growth. God wants you to receive His Son with all your heart through faith.

A–*__Always pray__*. This will allow you to spend more time with God. *__Admit__* to God that you are a sinner. *__Repent__*, turning away from your sin.

B–*__Believe__* that Jesus is God's Son and *__accept__* God's gift of forgiveness from sin. Bible reading every day is recommended in getting to know God.

C –*__Confess your faith__* in Jesus Christ as your Savior and Lord. Church attendance is critical to get plugged in to a local Bible-based and -believing church. This will surround you with other Christians

---

[19] Linder, Andrew, "4 Vital Ingredients for Staying Married"

who can guide you. There is no perfect church; however, there are understanding and passionate Christians who will stand in the gap when difficult times arise. They will inspire you to grow in Christ. To grow in Christ, you must live for Him and not let sin win. Growing in Christ means to increase your knowledge of Christ as you become more persistent in your love for Him and your obedience to Him.

Develop spiritual growth by believing and trusting that Jesus is living in and through you. Galatian 3:11 says, "But that no man is justified by the law in the sight of God is evident, for 'the just shall live by faith.'"

Communication is vital in your marriage relationship, as well as your relationship with Christ. God communicates with us through the Bible, revealing His character and His will. 2 Timothy 3:16-17 says, "All Scripture is given by inspiration of God, and is profitable for doctrine, for reproof, for correction, for instruction in righteousness, that the man of God may be perfect, thoroughly furnished unto all good work."

Prayer is another way of communicating with God, in which you can share your needs and your desire to do His will. Philippians 4:6-7 tells us, "Be careful for nothing, but in everything by prayer and supplication, with thanksgiving, let your requests be made known unto God; and the peace of God, which passeth all understanding, shall keep your hearts and minds through Christ Jesus."

Communicating with Christians also encourages you and others in faith. Hebrews 10:24-25 says, "And let us consider one another to provoke unto love and to good works: and forsaking the assembling of ourselves together, as the manner of some is; but exhorting one another; and so much the more, as ye see the day approaching."

As a follower of Christ, it is important to communicate with non-Christians to help them find Christ. Acts 4:12 says, "Neither is there salvation in any other: for there is none other name under heaven given among men, whereby we must be saved." In 1 Corinthians 3:6-7, the Bible states, "I have planted, Apollos watered; but God gave the increase. So then neither is he that planteth anything, neither he that watereth, but God that giveth the increase."

God is the source of your growth. You cannot become spiritually mature by trying to live without Him. As you walk in the power of the Holy Spirit, read the Bible, pray, tell people about Christ, and spend time with other believers, God will be at work in you, producing fruitfulness and maturity.

Chapter Ten

Bible Verses For Love And Marriage (NKJV)

LOVE	**MARRIAGE**
1 Corinthians 16:14	Ephesians 5:25
1 Corinthians 13:13	Ephesians 4:32
1 Peter 4:8	Proverbs 31:10
1 John 4:8	Mark 10:9
1 John 2:9-10	Galatians 5:13
Romans 12:9-10	1 Thessalonians 3:12

Acknowledgements

I would like to start by thanking my wonderful husband, Larry, for his input and support during the time of writing this book. I appreciate the testimony he wrote on how to treat a wife. He tells a story about his forty-six years of marriage to his late wife, who became gravely ill and required twenty-four-hour care for the last ten years. He was by her side, holding her hand until she took her last breath.

I would like to thank my daughter, Nicole, for her assistance and moral support with the editing. Thanks to others who are important to me for their contribution in sharing their testimonies.

Andrew Jackson
Donnell Powell
Dorothy Jackson
Glen Mitchell
Jimmy Bynum
Larry Oates
Linda Williams
Mary Raphillar

Mary Thomas
Mercades Mitchell
Muriel Bynum
Nadine Clipper
Nicole Jones
Odessa Bess
Ruth Hart
Valerie Dyson

Bibliography

Ash, Christopher, "Biblical View of Marriage" (The Gospel Coalition, 2020), Available from *https://thegospelcoalition.org/essay/biblical view marriage/*.

Best, Odessa, "Marriage Poem," 2017.

Bible Info, "What Does the Bible Say About Marriage," 2020, Available from *https://www.bibleinfo.com./en/questions/w…*

Brisco, Stuart, "God's Design for Marriage" 2019, Available from *https://www.tellingthetruth.org/read/individual/gods-design-for-marriage/*.

Burton, Neel, MD, "Hide and Seek:" The Psychology of Self-Deception-Kindle edition, *https://www.amazon.com/Hide-SeekSelf…Neel Burton…dp/B0079QQJLK.*

Chatel, Amanda, "The Real Difference Between Infatuation and Love," 2018.

Bustle.com/p/the-difference-between-lust-infatuati…

Hefferman, Carol, God's Design for Marriage, 2020 Available from *https://www.timothycenter.com/post/god-s-design-for-marriage-1.*

Kieda, Alyson, "Made For Each Other," Our Daily Bread, June, July, August 2020, *Daily Bread.org.*

Linder, Andrew, **"**4 Vital Ingredients for Staying Married,"[19] 2018, All Pro Dad. *https://www.allprodad. com/4-vital-ingredients-for-staying-married/.*

Marriage/The Marriage Creed, "Love Never Fails," 2013,

marriage- *miracles.blogspot.com2013/01/the-marri.*

Meredith, Don and Sally, "Biblical Perspective on Marriage. 2003

google.com/amp/s/www.crosswalk.com/ family/marr...

Overstreet, Elizabeth, "Questions to Ask Before Getting Married" 2018

*https://elizabethoverstreet. com/*2018/07/10-important-que...

Parker, Ken and Kay, "The ABC's of Becoming a Christian"

https://www.lifeway.com/en/contributors...

Rainey, Dennis and Barbara, by "Family Life," Copyright @2002.

https://www.familylife.com/podcast/gue...

Rainey, Dennis, "What Should Be the Husband's Role in Marriage," 2011.

https://www.familylife.com/articles/topics/
marriage/staying...

The Knot: Wedding | Wedding Planning Website
Inspiration, 1997-2020. https://www.theknot.
com/content/bible-verses-about-marriage

Walking Free: Recipe for a Godly Marriage, "The
Great Family Cookbook Project," 2004-2020).

https://wendywalkingfree.blogspot.com/2013/02/
recipe-for-godly-marriag...

White, Ellen G., "Testimonies Relative to Marriage
Duties,"

Ministry Magazine.org/archive/1969/03/ellen-
g.-whi... (1969/2003) Pamphlet.

White, Ellen G, "The Adventist Home," Section
5-From the Marriage Alta, Chapter 15-Solemn
Promises. 2020.

m.egwwritings.org/en/book/128.413

White, Ellen G., "tissue fabric, but a texture
that has borne the wear and tear and test
and trial of time." ***Mind, Character, and
Personality***, Vol 1

m.egwwritings.org/en/book77.785

CPSIA information can be obtained
at www.ICGtesting.com
Printed in the USA
BVHW030559250121
598668BV00001B/12